in the
City

Magic in the City

The True Power of Nature

Tudorbeth

Tudorbeth © 2013

All rights reserved.
No parts of this publication may be reproduced, stored in a retrieval system, or transmitted in any form or by any means whatsoever without the prior permission of the publisher.

A record of this publication is available from the British Library.

ISBN 978-1-907203-81-7

Typesetting by Wordzworth Ltd
www.wordzworth.com

Cover design by Titanium Design Ltd
www.titaniumdesign.co.uk

Printed by Lightning Source UK
www.lightningsource.com

Cover images by Nigel Peace

Published by Local Legend
www.local-legend.co.uk

*Dedicated to Lizzy who is the empress of earth magic, of fairies in the garden, nature, love, the Green Man, Yggdrasils, bluebells and snowdrops.
You have so much magic.*

Thank you and Blessed Be.

About this book

Magic has a new lease of life! In past times its practitioners were often vilified and persecuted. Yet Wicca is the oldest natural religion in the world and the Craft has never been forgotten, continuing in secret.

Meanwhile, our fascination with all things magical and mysterious has grown unabated, even despite the advances of science. From the nineteenth century to the present day, stage illusionists have drawn huge crowds. The paranormal has never been more popular, with a succession of books, films and television programmes.

And now at last, in this enlightened New Age, witchcraft can emerge from the broom closet and show us the true meaning of magic.

In this astonishing book, the fourth in her ground-breaking series, Tudorbeth teaches us the traditional secrets of numerology and herbalism, how to read tea leaves and how to invite the gods and goddesses to bring miracles into our everyday lives. This ancient knowledge has never before been offered with such simplicity and clarity.

The Author

Tudorbeth is a hereditary practitioner of the Craft. The rules and gifts of herb lore, scrying, healing, tasseomancy, numerology and candle magic have been passed down to her through several Celtic and English generations. Born in Wiltshire, she has an Honours degree in Religious Studies and has lived and worked in California and Italy, before returning to live in north London.

Previous Publications

The Craft in the City (ISBN 978-1-907203-43-5)

The Witch in the City (ISBN 978-1-907203-63-3)

Spells in the City (ISBN 978-1-907203-70-1)

To come in this series

Spirit in the City

Contents

Introduction	1
Magical Numbers	3
Magic and Symbols	15
Magic and Music	23
The Magical Battle of Britain	27
Magical Herbs and Teas	31
Tasseomancy Symbols	39
Earth Magic ~ Herbs	47
Masks	55
Dream Symbols	59
The Green Man	63
The Yggdrasil	71
Magic and Miracles	75
Gods and Goddesses of Magic	81
The Last Word	91
Suppliers of Excellent Resources as used by Tudorbeth	93

Introduction

Dear Reader,

In this book we are going to explore how magic is used within the Craft. We shall look at the tools and resources we use in our magical work and delve deeper into some lesser known methods. We shall also look at the practices and beliefs that we adhere to.

Magic is everywhere and in many different forms; every culture has its own magic, from Celtic to African, from Indian to Chinese. Magic is in the natural order of things. Indeed, all world religions have an element of magic within them. It is a little known fact that the term 'hocus pocus' was once used by Catholic priests to confuse the masses when speaking in Latin during the Eucharist: "Hoc est corpus meum." Nowadays, hocus pocus means trickery!

Yet true magic is not trickery, it is the current that carries the Craft throughout life and those who follow the Craft feel its pull throughout our lives and especially at certain times of the year. We swim in the flow of that magic, we believe in its power.

This book focuses on the Earth and the magic in the world around us, from herbs to trees to magical teas. In nature we seem to see magic more clearly. We see it in the weather, in a storm, in a rainbow, in the sunset or a red sky, in a dark night and in a full moon. What distinguishes witches, or practitioners of the Craft, from most of the rest of society is that we are beings of nature and we believe in magic. We embrace it in order to work for the good of all, to help nature in all its strife and in all its many beautiful and varied forms.

Moreover, for us magic has another unseen element, the presence of spirit in nature. Magic is that which binds us both to the Earth and to the higher realms, the realms of spirit.

We use magic to manifest our needs and desires. By consecration and invocation through spells and symbols we can charm, create and manifest those needs and desires. And we do not only manifest things; we can also pull things away from us - through execration and evocation we command the extraction of negative forces from us. This can only be done with a strong belief in magic and, as we are beings of nature, with the utmost belief in ourselves.

All the activities and tasks in this book can be carried out wherever you are, whether in the town, city or countryside. Magic is a part of you, so it goes wherever you go and lives wherever you live. It appears to us in different forms; we see it in the image of the Green Man staring out at us from a cathedral, or in the image of a stag on a city building. It is all around us, quietly waiting to be needed once again.

Just a word of warning! Always be careful to whom you disclose your magical practices, for even today not everyone is open-minded. Be especially careful if you go abroad, for in many parts of the world people are still persecuted for being witches or working with magic. In 2007 in Israel, a coffee reader was charged with practising magic...

Yet magic is beautiful so enjoy it, being respectful of all.

Blessed Be

Magical Numbers

Dear Reader,

In my earlier book *The Craft in the City*, I showed how to use the Magical Square of the Sun to draw down the power of the sun even on a dark winter's day. We also saw how to use it to make magic sun salt which in turn is used to make holy water.

Magical squares are a wonderful resource that we cannot be without. They originated thousands of years ago and are predominantly Hebrew and Arabic in origin. They found their way to us via the Crusades and other ventures into the East. In modern terms they are a bit like Sudoku, with numbers that add up to the same sum whichever way you add them, perpendicularly, horizontally or diagonally.

My 'old school' tradition believes that magic and Mathematics run parallel to one another. Indeed, many ancient philosophers were both mathematicians and alchemists, and breaking the codes of magic and other secrets was their mission. The power that resides in numbers, equations and formulae are synonymous with the mystical incantations of those who have gone before.

Everything in this world is connected by numbers and magic. People have two eyes, one mouth, ten fingers and so on. Ice crystals have six sides, spiders have eight legs and thus it goes on in the natural world. Numbers give identity and therefore each number has a character of its own.

Furthermore, each number has a magic of its own and as practitioners of the Craft we connect to the magic by knowing the power of each number. In spell work, the number of items used or the number of lines in a spoken spell are all important. For example, many of my own spells add up to five lines; they may have five items or the quantities may add up to five. This is because five is the number of the pentagram, our most sacred symbol, a symbol of power and protection within the Craft [1]. Five is the number of balance and it is also regarded as the number of health, vitality and light. Therefore, it is used quite a lot in my spells and rituals.

6	32	3	34	35	1
7	11	27	28	8	30
24	14	16	15	23	19
13	20	22	21	17	18
25	29	10	9	26	12
36	5	33	4	2	31

The Magical Square of the Sun
This is written out on yellow card or paper. Place a bowl of sea salt on top and leave it outside from sunrise to sunset.
Use this salt for cleansing and spell-weaving.

---

[1] See *The Witch in the City* for a detailed description of the pentagram and its meaning.

Many magical squares originated in the East, with letters of the Hebrew and Arabic alphabets given numbers, though there are several others. Some of them, if rewritten in their original letters, would form the names of God or of Alpha and Omega. Each magical square had a purpose; it was either a love charm, to connect with spirits, to see the future or to reveal the past. Some magical squares even helped women through pregnancy and childbirth.

Apart from the Magical Square of the Sun, there is another that I use often. If you add the numbers of this square perpendicularly, horizontally or diagonally, they all make thirty-four. If you add three and four together you get seven. In numerology, seven is a very good, powerful and protective number. It is often viewed as 'the number of magic', the number of witchcraft itself. Seven is regarded as lucky in many countries, such as Spain and Italy, where they believe that cats have seven lives rather than nine. There were seven Wonders of the Ancient World. The opposite faces of a die add up to seven – ah, Maths again! Seven days of creation, seven deadly sins and at the same time seven virtues. There's the seven-year itch and the seven major chakra points of the human body. In folklore it is said that a seventh son will be a werewolf, or that after six daughters the seventh child will be a son who will be a werewolf. Other European folklores disagree, believing that the seventh son of a seventh son is always a magical, mystical child with great power for healing and clairvoyance. Again, some say that the seventh son of a seventh son is a vampire. Vampires and werewolves... yes, I know!

However, in the Craft the number seven is a number of divinity: truth, love, power and protection. Indeed, the number seven is the Craft itself. There are many more meanings for the number seven and I suggest you do your own research and see how powerful this number is. Further, while doing so you will realise how powerful all numbers actually are and that Mathematics and magic are simply two sides of the same power.

6 | MAGIC IN THE CITY

Here is my favourite and mystical magical square - the square of thirty-four and of seven – also known as the Square of Jupiter.

4	14	15	1
9	7	6	12
5	11	10	8
16	2	3	13

The Square of Jupiter

Write or type out the square and if possible laminate it, as you will use it for many different things. It is surprising that of all the magical squares we know, this is one of the smallest, while Jupiter is the largest planet in the solar system and is regarded as the planet of expansion. However, think again of its numbers and their meanings, remembering that seven is the most powerful number of magic. This square can be used for many things such as protection, travel, good luck, to focus energy, for healing and more.

Magic cherry tea

There is one use in particular that I recommend, the making of magic cherry tea. Boil a kettle of water and pour it into a teapot, adding 1 tablespoon of cherry jam, 1 teaspoon of honey and 1 slice of lemon; give it a stir and place the pot on top of the magical square. Now stir three times and, as you do so, ask for the magical square to heal you of whatever your ailment or bad feeling is. For example, if you need an energy boost say:

Square of divine, heal me please,
My energy is low and my body is tired.
Give me ease.
So mote it be.

Pour the cherry tea and drink it slowly, imagining it healing you and infusing you with energy and strength.

Cherries are one of those wonderful fruits that have lots of rich goodness in them. Native Americans knew the power and health benefits of them and they were often used in healing potions. We now know that cherries have anti-inflammatory benefits, aid recovery, contribute to a healthy heart function and also promote restful sleep. This tea works best if you have made the jam yourself as you will know exactly what is in it and that it is free of additives. Bottling jams and preserves is a good way of keeping fruit all year round, though nothing could ever compete with actual fresh fruit.

Magical squares are a good source for drawing down energy and further power in the Craft. You are centralising the energy into your goal, ritual or spell. The Magical Square of the Sun above has numbers that add up to one hundred and eleven. This number is powerful in itself [2] but if we apply numerology to it, 1 + 1 + 1 = 3. Incidentally, in Hebrews 11:1 it is written: "Faith is being sure of what we hope for. It is being certain of what we do not see." Is this not a fundamental principle of the Craft? We do not see magic per se, yet it is something that is in everything.

The magic of numbers is very powerful and three is a wonderful number. It represents magic and creativity. It is also past, present and future and therefore a time identifier. It has many spiritual connections with mind, body and soul. Furthermore, three pertains specifically to the three faces of the

---

[2] It appears in several mathematical calculations, the product of two primes, 3 x 37. It is also regarded with superstition in several sports!

common Craft: Maiden, Mother and Crone. Many of us will have certain numbers that seem to dominate our lives, and mine are seven and three. How many times have you heard the saying, 'Everything happens in threes'?

Numbers have so much power in our lives; look back and see which number seems to dominate your life the most. It is certainly one to have on your lottery ticket! How long have you lived in a certain place or house before you moved? What have been your house numbers? Which numbers do you notice most often? For larger numbers, use numerology to condense them down to a single digit or to a significant number such as eleven or thirteen. (229 for example becomes 2 + 2 + 9 = 13.) So much negativity is written about thirteen and yet for many people it is lucky. Write your special numbers in your Book of Shadows, the record of all your magical work.

Your numerological 'Destiny Number' is based on your birthdate. For example, someone born on 7th March, 1972, has a destiny number of 11 because 7 + 3 + 1 + 9 + 7 + 2 = 29, and 2 + 9 = 11.

Here are the meanings of the numbers 1 to 9 and also the 'Master Numbers' 11 and 22. Which one represents you?

ONE
The number of leadership and individuality. However, when it comes to material matters this number can suffer fluctuations of fortune in early life, though by the later years stability is emphasised and number ones generally have their dreams of material wealth come true.

TWO
This is passive and receptive. Number two people can at times be easily led by less honest people than themselves. Number twos work best in partnerships and in contact with the public.

THREE
The number of luck and of creativity. These people can have unrealistic ideas; however, their optimism usually works out as they make substantial gains.

FOUR
The number of hard work and of a serious nature. Number four people are very committed and relish the new challenges they have to face.

FIVE
This is the number of adventure. Number five people do not lack initiative, but they may lack staying power. Number fives have a constantly restless disposition.

SIX
The number of love and harmony. Number six people seek harmony and are very sociable and considerate.

SEVEN
The number of the mystic and also of magic. Number seven people have uncanny luck in grasping opportunities when they arise and turning them to their advantage.

EIGHT
This is the number of material success. Number eight people are practical, reliable and are content to make slow progress. Number eights have the patience and perseverance to overcome all obstacles.

NINE
The number of the visionary. The number nine is associated with enterprise and initiative. Number nines are confident and courageous, though they may also take unnecessary risks which unfortunately do not always come off.

ELEVEN
This is a Master Number and symbolises creative energy. This number holds the promise of worldly success. If it is your Destiny Number then teaching and the media is your lifestyle path to choose. Eleven may also be condensed further to a single digit, 1 + 1 = 2.

TWENTY-TWO
This is the other Master Number of numerology. It relates to perfection, the number of the idealist, and people with this number will strive for an important cause. They will act selflessly to help others less fortunate and strive for the equality of all. Twenty-two may also be seen as 2 + 2 = 4.

All numbers have meaning and power that reside within you always; your life number is never going to change. If you are interested in numerology then this might be your specialism so research it.

For many in the Craft, numbers have a symbolic function revealing to us the nature of the universe. This thought can lead not only to numerology but also to Hermetic thought and to arithmology, which is a metaphysical form of Mathematics. Some of us take that further and delve into the arithmology of Plato, Pythagoras or the Cabbala. Magic and numbers play a part in the Craft today just as they have done in the past.

Yet it is the essence of magic that it is within numbers that concerns us here. Numbers are everywhere in our lives, we cannot survive without them in one form or another, from the ticking hands of a clock to the money we receive for our hard work. If you have worked out which numbers seem to dominate your life then let us use them on a lottery ticket, channel that energy and see if we can delve into the magic of the universe!

The Lottery Spell
Buy your lottery ticket and by the light of a gold candle say this spell over it:

> *Be it light, be it right.*
> *Numbers reveal your magic tonight.*
> *Show me the numbers to draw.*
> *Show me the money more.*
> *Create the magic of lottery.*
> *An' it harm none, so mote it be.*

After you have discovered your own life number and the numbers that seem to prevail in your life, try making your own magical square. It is the physical resource of your own magic and power. Magic is within you so your magical square with your own personal numbers is sacred to you and only you. Write your magical square in your Book of Shadows. It can be as small as needs be but remember that it is your magic and yours alone. Have this magical square present whenever you cast circles or send healing.

There is another way of finding a life number, by using the numbers of your name. In numerology, all letters have a number associated with them. (Remember that the origin of magical squares was to 'encode' the name of the Divine, or the incantation of a spell.)

Here is how to convert the alphabet into numbers:

1	2	3	4	5	6	7	8	9
A	B	C	D	E	F	G	H	I
J	K	L	M	N	O	P	Q	R
S	T	U	V	W	X	Y	Z	

This is often referred to as 'the Pythagorean Code'. You simply add up the numbers relating to the letters in your name. For example:

T	U	D	O	R	B	E	T	H	
2 +	3 +	4 +	6 +	9 +	2 +	5 +	2 +	8	= 41

and 4 + 1 = 5

Therefore the Life Number for Tudorbeth is five. However, one must add that this method is not as reliable or as true as your birthda te number. You can never change your birth date number so that gives your true number, whereas your name could easily change, by marriage, deed poll or simply by personal choice.

The Magical Square of the Future
We can also use numbers to foresee the future. Here is another version of the Square of Mars.

1	2	6
3	5	7
4	8	9

Write out the square on a large piece of paper or card, and on the back write the meanings of each number:

1 A new lover will be making an appearance soon.
2 Do not interfere with the affairs of others as it will rebound onto you.
3 It is just an infatuation and will lead to nothing.
4 Be aware of gossip as the information could be false.

5   Present feelings may change so do not sign up to any long-term commitments.
6   Your love is true. This is a lucky time for you.
7   A nasty surprise! Prepare for rejection.
8   Trust in those you love.
9   Ignore the gossip and do not give in to jealousy.

You could laminate the card and keep it for future reference. When you have a question, perhaps about a close relationship, place the square on a flat surface, close your eyes and ask the question. Holding a coin in your hands, meditate on the question, then with eyes still shut throw the coin onto the square. The number it lands on is your answer.

Enjoy your numbers and magical squares. Remember that numbers have a symbolism of their own and can open up hidden mysteries of the universe. However, as always a word of warning: if you research magical squares you will find that not all of them work with 'the light', so be careful to follow your own path and go where your own numbers lead.

In the next letter we shall look at other more common symbols of magic.

Blessed Be

Magic and Symbols

Dear Reader,

Magic is in everything and the intent with which we approach it reveals the power within. However, even though magic is within 'everything' there are a number of traditional symbols of magic.

One in particular is the bell which is said to drive away evil spirits. Bells were found throughout the ancient world, from Egypt to Pompeii. There are countless ornaments of bells, or candle holders which served a dual purpose of light and bell. People throughout history have believed that bells keep bad spirits away. In the Craft, bells are used to invoke the Goddess or to call the elementals such as fairies.

The pentagram is of course our most sacred and magical symbol. We always have it represented in some form in our houses or physically on our bodies at all times, or we trace it in the air to give us added protection when we need to draw down extra magic or power. The pentagram is explained in detail in *The Witch in the City* so we shall not go into it here. However, what must be said is that the pentagram is the epitome of magic.

Mirrors

Mirrors have often been a symbol of magic and power. Think about how many stories involve a mirror. One of the most famous involved Snow White's stepmother, an evil witch who had a magic mirror of which she would ask, "Who is the fairest of them all?" The oldest mirrors were pots of water, or the surfaces of rivers and streams. One of these captivated the young Narcissus who wasted away gazing into it, having seen his own reflection and fallen in love with himself.

Mirrors have often been used as a resource for finding an answer, from Snow White's stepmother to the scryers of the past. Nostradamus was one such famous scryer who used the water and bowl method to see the events of the future and thus write his quatrains of prophecy. Mirrors answer our questions and can be used not only for seeing how one looks today but also what can happen tomorrow. In other cultures, mirrors are not only used for magic but also for harmony of the environment, as in Feng Shui.

Many witches have their own scrying mirror and you could create your own. Buy a small mirror in a frame, such as a dressing table mirror, and place it on a piece of wood or hard cardboard on which you can now create your own frame with sea shells, playing cards, tarot symbols, zodiac symbols and so on. You would use sea shells if you are a water sign such as Pisces, Cancer or Scorpio. You could also use melted candle wax if you are a fire sign, or images of the sun, moon and stars. In fact, you can decorate the frame of the mirror in any way you like, the only rule being that it has to be something personal for you. This is your magic mirror and you are going to use it for a number of magical workings, from scrying to protection and healing spells. However, before you use it, infuse it with your magic and say this spell over your mirror:

> *Mirror, mirror on the wall,*
> *Let me see the future of all.*
> *Give me the sight.*
> *But do not fright.*
> *Mirror, mirror, enchant me.*
> *Mirror, mirror, so mote it be.*

Mirrors can be like doors looking through to another place and time. Think about the story of Alice Through the Looking Glass or the poem The Lady of Shallot, who uses a mirror to see Camelot. Many stories regarding mirrors tell us of other worlds and help us to see our world in a way that we may not normally be able to. Some mirrors, such as the Buddhist mirror of Dharma, reveal our past and our actions of the past. Mirrors are therefore useful tools of both magic and of sight.

They can show us what is good and also what could be termed 'soulless'. In folklore, both vampires and werewolves have no reflection, as the reflection is a symbol of the soul. Our Celtic ancestors were buried with mirrors, the women especially, as it was believed that mirrors could capture the soul and therefore keep it safe. It is this emphasis upon the soul that concerns us here - mirrors are believed to be indicators of spirit, and for warding off evil if hung in the house.

Also in our tradition there is something called 'the witch ball'. For all intents and purpose it looks like a silver bauble you would hang on the Christmas tree. Yet its origins are hundreds of years old. They gained popularity in the eighteenth century and were hung in windows to scare away witches, the theory being that an evil spirit would be frightened away by their own reflection. Some witch balls had strands of hair inside them and worked in a similar way to the dream catchers of Native Americans, entangling the evil that appears in nightmares.

Some may disagree with creating a witch ball. However, embracing that which was once deemed negative is a positive acknowledgment of our past. We now have the knowledge and love to realise how our history was made and we can reclaim it. If you would like to create a witch ball as a protection for your house, the easiest way is to buy a silver Christmas bauble. Try to choose one with well-polished sides so that you can see your reflection in it. Alternatively you could buy a silver, mini-mirrored disco ball and use that instead. Before you hang up your witch ball, light a silver candle and hold your silver ball in your hand, saying these words over it:

> *Hear me now.*
> *Power of the witches rise.*
> *Blessed ones, hear my cries.*
> *Let no-one enter who is foe,*
> *No-one with intentions of woe.*
> *Thank you all and Blessed Be.*
> *An' it harm none, so mote it be.*

Wind chimes

Wind chimes are symbols of magic, often used to ward off evil spirits. The earliest wind chimes from ancient Rome had bells attached to them to create the sound and in eastern societies bells were also used, hung in corners of the house to guard against evil. However, in Asia wind chimes are believed to be good luck and they are used in Feng Shui with the belief that they maximise the flow of chi and life's energy. Nowadays they are made of glass, bamboo, shells, stone, wood, metal tubes or porcelain, and there is a new wave of using recycled utensils such as silverware or even cookie cutters!

In Eastern Europe, wind chimes are used as indicators of when spirits are around. That is why many of us have wind chimes in the house: when they inexplicably move with no draught or window open, we know there are 'guests' around.

Try to create your own wind chimes made of items that are important to you. If you are a water sign you could make them from shells or if you have a number of crystals around you can use them too. The design can be quite basic. Use a round piece of metal, wood, plastic or even strong cardboard; it should look like a large ring as you are going to tie the items to it. You can use ribbon, string or twine to attach your items to the ring.

Cut some different lengths of ribbon but also some the same length so that the items can touch each other when the wind blows. Then tie the chimes up in your house or garden.

If you would like the elementals to feel welcome in your house, say the words below as you put your wind chimes up. The elementals are those beings of the earth, air, fire and water such as fairies, pixies, elves, salamanders or water sprites. (A full description of elementals can be found in *Spirit in the City*.)

> *Tinkling sounds,*
> *Items of my heart.*
> *Blessed elementals,*
> *Merry meet and merry part.*
> *Enter freely in my witch's den.*
> *And then depart freely again.*
> *So mote it be.*

Sigils

A sigil is a seal, a symbol used in magic and a pictorial signature. In the Christian era sigils were often associated with angels, demons and various other entities. Yet please look beyond this. You can create your own seal, your own symbol of magic which epitomises your power and your intent within the realm of magic. Sigil magic is quite fun and if you know shorthand it's even easier. Basically a sigil represents the desired outcome of a spell you might cast. As always, being precise regarding what you actually desire is of paramount importance.

Write down the spell and make it into one big sentence. Then reduce the sentence so that no letter is repeated (similar to shorthand in which you take out all the vowels of a word). For example, if I want more money:

> *To gain one hundred pounds,*
> *An' it harm none, so mote it be.*

This then becomes:

> *Togainehudrpsmb*

After you have condensed your sentence down, you now create the sigil by reducing these letters into shapes. Some can be upside down, on their side or back to front. You could even use 'magic mirror writing' - hold the mirror up to your shortened letter sentence and see what shapes the letters make. Then when you have redesigned the letters, make them all into a shape that you are happy with. Ideally, just like the pentagram they should be drawn in one single stroke.

Now draw a circle around your sigil to contain it, and place the intended outcome upon it. The energy you have used in creating this piece of magic is sacred and unique; it belongs to you and only to you. All your sigils should be kept in your Book of Shadows.

Have fun making your pictorial spells. Sigils are a truly beautiful piece of magic similar to mandalas, unique and powerful for focusing our energy and thoughts upon. Just a word of warning: do not use the example shown above as it is not very precise - instead of gaining one hundred pounds in money you may just gain one hundred pounds in weight! A full description of how to weave spells can be found in *Spells in the City*.

The Magic Circle
The circle shape is another magical symbol that we can call upon. The magic circle is the protective circle we draw when performing a ritual, casting a spell or sending healing, because a circle represents both spirit and matter.

Our ancestors built houses that were not square but round, because this gave more protection from the elements than a square house. A circular design was both flexible and strong with the ability to be safer in severe weather conditions. The circle is also found in nature, from trees to stones and the Earth itself, to the ovoid shape of eggs. Places like Stonehenge, Avebury and New Grange in Ireland are some of the oldest monuments in the world and have stood the test of time. To the ancients, magic was a part of their lives and the magic of a circle was a powerful force.

Traditionally when we cast a circle for ritual it should be nine feet in diameter. However, not all of us have room for creating such a generous amount of sacred space so you may use a smaller circle. Further, if you have very little space, you may just create an imaginary circle of protection around you. Create your own protective space either by spraying your holy water or sprinkling your magic moon salt around you. (These are described in both *The Witch in the City* and *The Craft in the City*.)

No matter how small your space, imagine you have a golden white light around you and say these words:

> *I cast the circle round and round,*
> *Forever protected, safe and sound.*
> *No harm, no negativity shall pass to me*
> *For I am safe within my circle round.*
> *An' it harm none, so mote it be.*

It is also worth noting here the importance of the circled dot. This symbol is synonymous with the sun in many contexts, for example from astronomy to alchemy, to ancient Egypt and to many languages and societies. It is a universal symbol of the absolute.

⊙ The dot itself represents the point of creation. It is both origin and conclusion and for us it represents the seed of potential. When placed in the centre of the hexagram, or Star of David, this represents the fifth element. For many cultures, an amulet with a circled dot is believed to protect against the evil eye.

There are many other symbols of magic but always look to your own culture or ancestry for your symbols. My symbols are from the north, such as the valknut and the triquetra (which some regard as the same).

The valknut is a symbol of Odin and is three interlocking triangles. It is regarded as a knot and is a protective symbol. The triquetra is also a symbol of protection and represents many aspects of the Craft, primarily maiden, mother and crone. Further, although the sign predates Christianity it has also been used as a symbol of the Holy Trinity. As with many magical symbols, the power comes with it being drawn without the pen leaving the paper, in one stroke.

There are countless other symbols of magic and these have been just a chosen few that are universal and used by practitioners of the Craft. They have been used throughout the world and at all times from past to present. Therefore, explore magical symbols for yourself and see which ones seem meaningful to you.

Blessed Be

Magic and Music

Dear Reader,

There is something wonderful about music - it is the auditory version of magic itself! The power of music to create a change of mood within us is simply awe-inspiring. One thing to remember is that the term music can also be translated as 'magic' or 'incantation', because music is captivating and therefore can be enchanting to those who hear it.

No other culture realised this more than ancient Greece. The story of Orpheus is a beautiful legend. Orpheus was a musician who played the lyre. In his music was magic; when he played he was able to charm all living beings, including animals and even the gods, in particular the god of the Underworld, Hades. Orpheus loved music second only to his wife Eurydice. They were blissfully happy but (as in all Greek legends) this happiness was not to last and Eurydice was killed by a viper's bite. Her soul was cast into the Underworld and Orpheus was so consumed with grief that he made his way to the Underworld to get Eurydice back. However, this was no easy feat as Hades was a tough god who did not fall for any sad story. Yet Orpheus was determined and in his music was all the love, pain and grief over the loss of his wife. As he played his music for Hades in the Underworld, all who listened were captivated; and in the shadows of the Underworld, someone else was listening to this beautiful music, Eurydice.

Hades was so moved and 'enchanted' by the sweet magical music that he allowed Eurydice to return to her husband, on condition that Orpheus had to walk out of the Underworld without glancing back to see if Eurydice was following behind him. However, as Orpheus was making his way out he began to doubt that his wife was following him. Just as he was reaching the end of the Underworld he turned back to see Eurydice had been following him all along; but suddenly, as Orpheus had broken the deal, Eurydice was snatched back by Hades. Curiosity got the better of man once again and, just like Pandora and Psyche, Orpheus lost his wife.

However, what this story shows us is the power of music and the way that it can even charm and enchant a tough god like Hades and bring him to tears. The sheer power of music can reduce any of us to tears. Music can also make us happy, it evokes memories of past times, lovers have their song, married couples dance to a special song at their wedding. Who does not feel better when playing music? It can change our mood, make us happy or make us sad.

Yet music in magical practices is not just used to enchant, it is also a way to raise the energy levels. In order to create a powerful spell, the energy needs to be strong in order for the spell to be cast or a healing to be successful. Whether it is from the beating of a drum, the haunting melodies of a flute or pan pipes, the shaman, witch or wise elder always uses music to begin a ritual. The same is true when music is played or we sing in a church. Music is used to create an atmosphere of positivity, love, energy and community.

Even for solitary practitioners of the Craft, we may have a musical instrument which we feel drawn to for raising our energy levels. The bell is used to invoke and draw down the Goddess, or we may just have music playing in the background while performing our ritual, casting a spell or sending some healing. The sound of the bell being rung can also disperse negative energies.

In Greek mythology the nine daughters of Zeus are called muses. The muses inspire mortals in the great works of art, with individual responsibilities for all aspects of the arts from drama even to astronomy. They are all adept at creating music, as music was such a powerful force in the ancient world. When your creative abilities have seemed to diminish, call upon one of the muses to help and guide you. Here is a list of their names and their correspondences.

The Nine Daughters of Zeus

Muse	Inspires	Colour	Stone	Oil	Symbols
Calliope	Epic poetry	Gold	Goldstone	Peach	Writing tablet
Clio	History	White	Diamond	Jasmine	Scrolls
Euterpe	Flutes and lyric poetry	Yellow	Citrine	Honeysuckle	Flute
Thalia	Comedy	Blue, cyan	Turquoise	Lotus	Comic mask
Melpomene	Tragedy	Grey	Haematite	Sandalwood	Tragic mask
Terpischore	Dance	Green	Emerald	Pine	Lyre
Erato	Love poetry	Pink, magenta	Rose quartz	Magnolia	Guitar
Polyhymnia	Sacred poetry	Red	Ruby	Frankincense	Veil
Urania	Astronomy	Black	Obsidian	Patchouli	Compass or globe

Further, when you are casting a spell and would like some extra help, you can also ask a muse to help you. Here is such a spell; just adapt the wording to fit your intention, e.g. a money spell, healing, a love spell, etcetera. Light a candle of the colour corresponding to the intention of the spell and say these words:

> *Oh sacred muse,*
> *Daughter of Zeus,*
> *Your music divine*
> *Grant this love/money spell of mine.*
> *An' it harm none, so mote it be.*

Whenever you are spell casting, think of your favourite piece of music, something that makes you happy. Put it on and dance to it, lift your spirits and raise your energy with it. Some spells themselves have rhymes and this gives them rhythm. A spell is more potent if it resonates to the heartbeat of the universe. We have rhythm within us from the moment we come into being; the beats of our hearts are a musical rhythm that resonates throughout our lives, so play music and listen to your own music within.

You should now be in the right frame of mind to cast some spells or send some healing to a friend or loved one in need. Light the appropriate candle: blue for healing, green for money, pink for love, etcetera. Cast your circle and say your spells, keeping the music on in the background while you do your ritual. Even in meditation we can have music playing. It can be any kind of music, whatever suits your mood or what you feel matches your magical working of the day. You choose for you are the shaman now, you are the wise one, you are the witch.

Blessed Be

The Magical Battle of Britain

Dear Reader,

At certain points throughout our history, magic has shown its force. It appears at times of great strife. The Second World War was one such time. People were worried about the threat of a German invasion and many had lost loved ones. People turned to faith, to their churches, some to Spiritualism and some turned to the ancestors of the past. Thus begins one of the best stories regarding magic and witchcraft in Britain, known as the Magical Battle of Britain.

It is hard for us to imagine what it must have been like for our parents and grandparents during those times, despite what the films would have us believe. There were the bombings, the blitz, the night-time raids over our major cities with buildings and streets in ruins, blackouts, and rationing of what was available to eat or buy. It must have been very daunting to walk past those bombsites knowing that neighbours, friends or family had lived there. People turned to religion for hope, and faith in God and in each other was strong.

There are some key names regarding the Magical Battle of Britain but no other stands out amongst the rest more than Dion Fortune. She was a remarkable woman given the time she was living in and one of our rare visionaries. Through a series of weekly letters to her students during 1939 to 1942, she instructed the members of her magical order, the Fraternity of the Inner Light, to visualise angelic protection over Britain and to give the British strength while under fire. One must remember that for those living in those times it really was a case of the forces of light fighting the forces of darkness.

In London Underground stations there were posters of the circle of light with a cross in the centre. The belief in Spiritualism, magic and the angelic forces of good was real and the presence of magic was experienced on a far greater level than ever recorded. The whole nation worked together including those who lived and walked the path of magic. It has become a part of our folklore that during 1939 to 1942 the potential threat of invasion by Germany was fought not only on the physical plane with the Army, Royal Navy and Royal Air Force, but also on the spiritual plane with magic.

The witches of England, from the covens of the New Forest to the witches of Lincolnshire, went to the sea and performed a protection spell. This spell was so powerful, reinforced with the power of the sea, that it created a spiritual force field around Britain. It was similar to when we create a protective shield around ourselves but on a much larger scale. The energy, power and magic that were involved in this type of spell must have been incredible. Yet the threat of invasion was so great that everyone was expected – and wanted - to do their part. As history has shown, for whatever reason Hitler did not invade Britain and instead turned his attention towards the Soviet Union. His own advisors could not understand why he changed his strategy then.

The Magical Battle of Britain was fought here by men and women who believed in magic. The war raged until 1945 with the estimated dead of up to about seventy million. It is little wonder that the effects of the war can still be felt today. And there are places in our cities that were bombed and in which has been created what we call a vortex – pockets of complete destruction which have an 'atmosphere' to them. There may be new buildings, shopping centres or car parks over these bombsites now, but there is still an atmosphere within them, a vortex that has been opened and never closed. When you believe in magic and work with it, you will begin to realise and understand why a certain place creates negative thoughts in you.

If you would like to give thanks to the brave men and women who fought in the Magical Battle of Britain, here is a blessing of Remembrance. Light a white candle and say these words:

> *Ancestors, reveal your ancient past,*
> *May you find peace at last.*
> *Your love, strength and bravery*
> *Gave us the chance to be free.*
> *Thank you for all you have done,*
> *Your grace, your sacrifice for everyone.*
> *Thank you to one and all.*
> *May you find peace for evermore.*
> *Ancestors, Blessed Be.*

Leave the candle burning for as long as you can, allowing it to burn itself out, or extinguish it in the usual way if you are not able to keep an eye on it.

There is much written about the Magical Battle of Britain and I suggest you research it further, as it truly is a fascinating part of our history.

Blessed Be

Magical Herbs and Teas

Dear Reader,

Herbs and their magical properties have been discussed in detail in both *The Witch in the City* and in *Spells in the City*. Therefore, here we shall look specifically into the wonder and magic that is herbal tea. Tea can be both medicinal, as it is healing to us, but it is also a social event. It can be a meal in itself, with the Afternoon Tea that developed in the late eighteenth century. In other parts of the world, the preparation and drinking of tea is regarded as a ritual.

Sometimes we need to recharge our batteries and nothing better than a cup of tea will do. Traditionally tea is made from the leaves of the tea plant and is believed to have originated in China. Yet we have always made hot drinks with herbs for medicinal purposes, sweetened with our favourite spices or honey. It is a well-known fact that an infusion of ginger, hot water and lemon is ideal for coughs and colds. And we are finding out now that Green Tea may help reduce the risk of heart disease and also some forms of cancer. Tea in general contains L-Theanine which is associated with producing a calm but alert mental state (by affecting the brain's alpha waves), which is probably why so many of us have it as our first drink of the day. Wake up to tea and a good morning!

However, if you would like to create your own tea for a personal boost, especially one corresponding to your star sign, below are some potential flavours you could use. You can buy loose green or black tea leaves and add the dried fruits and flowers pertaining to your star sign to produce the tea you desire. You might be surprised! This might indicate which planets are more prevalent in your birth chart if you do not like your assumed star sign's taste.

Light a gold candle, pour the tea pertaining to your star sign and say this spell as you slowly sip your tea:

Universe of light,
Planets of my birth,
Give me strength to fight.
The days are long and hard.
Replenish my strength with this tea.
An' it harm none, so mote it be.

Star Sign	Planet	Herbs	Flowers and plants	Vegetables	Fruits
Aries	Mars	Honeysuckle, cowslip, rosemary	Poppy, holly, geranium, thistle	Onion	Orange, pineapple
Taurus	Venus	Elder, lovage, spearmint	Violet, rose, daisy, lily	Potato	Apple, apricot
Gemini	Mercury	Lavender, hare's foot, fern	Woodbine, lavender, lily of the valley	Carrot	Raspberry, fig, date, passion fruit
Cancer	Moon	Saxifrage, hyssop, balm	Water lily, wild flowers, marigold, willow	Lettuce	Pear, pineapple
Leo	Sun	Bay, borage, angelica, cinnamon	Daffodil, sunflower, chamomile, citrus trees	Pumpkin	Orange, lemon
Virgo	Mercury	Caraway, myrtle, fennel	Small flowers, fennel, barley wheat	Carrot	Raspberry, plum
Libra	Venus	Daisy, garden mint	Pansy, orchid, white rose, vine	Potato	Apple, peach

Star Sign	Planet	Herbs	Flowers and plants	Vegetables	Fruits
Scorpio	Pluto, Mars	Broom, hops, basil	Heather, blackthorn, rhododendron	Jerusalem artichoke, onion	Pomegranate, pineapple, dark red grape
Sagittarius	Jupiter	Moss, sage, dandelion	Lime, oak, mulberry, pink	Asparagus	Blueberry, banana
Capricorn	Saturn	Comfrey, hemlock, beet	Pine, ivy, carnation, black poppy	Beetroot	Coconut, pear
Aquarius	Saturn, Uranus	Sorrel, quince, heart's ease	Myrrh, orchid, most fruit trees, frankincense	Beansprout, beetroot	Strawberry, coconut, rhubarb
Pisces	Jupiter, Neptune	Dock, sage, fig	Water lily, willow tree, moss, fern	Asparagus, mushroom	Blueberry, melon, cherry, almond

Aries

The reasons for many of these correspondences is that they relate not only to which planet rules a particular sign but also to which element is associated. Aries is a fire sign, for example, and Aries people often enjoy citrus flavours of the sun, so the orange is perfect for them.

Taurus

This is an earth sign and Taureans have a natural love of food, with acute taste buds sensitive to subtleties of flavour, texture and colour. Therefore, apricots are a good earthy fruit for them.

Gemini

Geminis are ruled by Mercury and love anything that is exotic or unusual so fig, passion fruit and dates are ideal for these quick-thinking, excellent communicators.

Cancer
Cancer is a water sign. Its people have a sweet tooth yet also like savoury things. The pineapple is a fruit which can be used in both sweet and savoury dishes.

Leo
Lovely sunny Leos love anything with a lemony flavour. Therefore lemons and sweet spices such as cinnamon are perfect for this sign.

Virgo
An earth sign of practicality, generally Virgo people prefer savoury foods. But they often prefer quite piquant foods like pickled onions and vinegar. Therefore a simple but perfect plum is ideal for Virgo, as is the bittersweet cranberry.

Libra
Libra is an air sign, symbolised by the scales of justice, so of course a balanced diet is a must. If Librans indulge one day they will eat lightly the next. That is why the peach is an ideal fruit for Libra. The peach is not quite a citrus and not quite a berry either, a unique in-between. A bit like a Libran.

Scorpio
Sensual Scorpio people love anything that is deep, dark and mysterious. So deep, dark red or even black grapes are perfect for them.

Sagittarius
Easy-going and adventurous Sagittarians generally like food for its energy-giving properties. The banana is good for those constantly on the go.

Capricorn

Capricorns are a lovely, loyal earth sign who have a sensible down-to-earth approach to food. The humble but delicious pear is just right for them.

Aquarius

Aquarian people love food that is different and original, a bit like them. They may have strange tastes, like eating cheese and pickles with strawberry jam. The strawberry is ideal for Aquarians since it can be used as an accompaniment to something else.

Pisces

At the first sign of the spring, think of the festivals that are celebrated at that time. One of them is the Cherry Blossom Festival which usually begins in March. Pisces folk are always on hand to offer tea and sympathy. This is the sign of the true tea drinker, the tea-and-cake person. The tastes of cherries and almonds are perfect for them.

The other wonderful thing about teas is that you can make specific ones for the seasons. As you drink your winter tea, spring tea, summer tea and autumn tea, imagine the strength and power of that season pouring into you. Spring brings renewal and growth, while summer is in full bloom and strength; autumn brings the changes of vibrant colour and winter brings rest and the quiet planning for another year. If we break it down to one word, spring is energy, summer is strength, autumn is adaptation and winter is rest.

The other magical use for tea is the wonderful art of tasseomancy, or tea-reading. People have read tea leaves for hundreds of years and tasseomancy as such developed in the seventeenth century. Of course, tea leaves are not the only things that can be used to foresee the future - coffee grounds, wine sediments and even melted wax are some of the other items that have been used in different parts of the world at different times. In ancient Greece, a divination practice called 'kottabos' involved throwing the remains of a cup of wine into a metal bowl. The shapes of the wine and sediment settling in the bowl were read for omens. It was believed that the gods sent messages this way in order to warn and instruct humans. Coffee-reading is done mainly in Turkey, Serbia and Greece, countries that predominantly drink coffee. Tea-reading became especially popular in the United Kingdom.

However, in some places throughout the world tasseomancy is still a crime. Yet it is a truly wonderful gift and, if you have it, congratulations to you. There are no words really to describe what it is like other than that a true reader of the tea leaves will literally see the shapes 'jump out' to them in the cup; sometimes they may even glow. The standard shapes all have meanings and there are literally hundreds of symbols to understand, but at the end of this letter there is a glossary of meanings for you to practise with.

Someone who is not a natural reader will have to look for the shapes, although you can be taught to understand them. As with all magic, some things will come easily while you will need to work at others. It's just the same as anything in life - we all need to be taught the basics. Not everyone is a natural dancer, but those who aren't do not have to give up; if they still enjoy dancing and want to dance, they put the hard work in. Magic is just like that. Some things will come to you and some things you will struggle with.

Tea-reading is an art that is passed from one generation to the next, although it may not take effect with one generation and may skip one until it find the right person. It is the magical calling that determines a true tea-reader, and though magic is within all of us, women are still leading the way in this.

If you would like to try your hand at tea-reading then make a cup of tea with loose tea of a flavour of your choice. There are many techniques associated with this that differ from family to family; generally you are supposed to make the tea in a pot and then drink it until there is just a little left in the bottom of the cup. You then swill the tea round and see what shapes appear.

The kind of tea to be used is always loose leaf. The pot ideally should have a wide spout. The cup itself should have a broad top and bottom and be white inside, not patterned. Mugs are not good to use as you cannot see the symbols properly. The person wanting the reading must drink the tea until there is about half a teaspoon of tea left. Then, holding the cup in your left hand, swirl it round quickly three times anti-clockwise and turn the cup upside down onto the saucer, leaving it to drain. The reader will then pick it up after a couple of minutes. You may like to say these words:

> *Blessed leaves we read tonight,*
> *Grant me the gift of foresight.*
> *Show me the plans of future sights.*
> *Show me all the good and right.*
> *An' it harm none, so mote it be.*

In many families the customs and traditions of tasseomancy are passed on and there is a whole range of lore pertaining to tea. For example, if there are lots of bubbles on the surface of the tea after it has been poured into the cup, then extra money is coming your way. Also, if there is a single leaf floating on the surface of the tea then money luck is yours, so buy a lottery ticket! There are different beliefs pertaining to where the tea leaves are, near the handle, at the bottom of the cup, near the rim and so on, even before one gets to the interpretation of the actual symbols.

Generally a tea-reading will only reveal short-term predictions, such as for a week or two and sometimes up to six months ahead though this is rare. But it is truly a magical art form which we should not lose. So enjoy your magical teas and try your hand at tasseomancy to see if you have the gift.

Blessed Be

Tasseomancy Symbols

A cross with a circle: Be patient as nothing can be achieved at present. Unfortunately, circumstances are against you.

Acorn: A positive symbol of health and future security. Success will come from hard work.

Aircraft: If it is opposite the handle of the cup then it means a journey. It can also mean news or visitors from abroad, a promotion or new project. However, if it is poorly formed it means hopes for immediate success will be frustrated.

Alligator: Enemies, danger. This is not a good sign!

Anchor: Success in business, good luck, prosperity and a secure relationship.

Angel: Good fortune, love and peace. It can also mean a guardian angel is looking out for you.

Antlers: A warning sign, so be careful about journeys, health, business and family.

Ape: A hidden enemy, gossip, so be careful what you say and to whom you say it.

Apple: Vitality, health, also good luck in business.

Arch: Wishes coming true, unexpected opportunities.

Arrow: News and important communication.

Axe: Stand up for yourself and problems will be overcome.

Baby: Perhaps a real baby is on the way, or a new business or new home.

Basket: A baby or a pet will be a new addition to the family. Finances may fluctuate.

Bat: Hard work and travel.

Bees: A good and happy sign. Expect to be busy in every area of your life.

Bell: Wedding news if there are two bells in a reading. Generally though, a bell means good news all round.

Birds: News from a distance. It can also mean journeys. Check your investments.

Bird's nest: A lucky find, a bargain, an antique.

Boat: A holiday – or a difficult time lies ahead if there are clouds with it.

Book: A secret will be revealed. If there is an initial with it then the enquirer will get to know a writer.

Boot: A change in a job or work situation, or at home.

Bouquet: A happy marriage, loyal friends.

Bridge: Happy, safe journeys.

Cabbage: Jealousy.

Car: Friends will be visiting.

Castle: Unexpected money luck.

Cat: Deception and lies.

Circles: If the circles are large then it means the end of an issue. If the circles are small, there will be news of a marriage.

Clock: A difficult time is now passing.

Clouds: Disappointment, doubts.

Clover, Shamrock: Prosperity.

Clown: A full and happy social life.

Crescent: New beginnings, opportunities and interests.

Crescent Moon: Romance.

Cross: Quarrels and problems.

Crown: Success.

Dagger: Slow down and be careful.

Dancers: Good news is on the way and life is changing for the better.

Dashes: Energy and a new project.

Dog: A lucky sign of true friendship and loyalty.

Dots: Money, a windfall, legacy or salary increase.

Dragon: Sudden changes but they will be positive.

Drum: Success, publicity - perhaps scandal.

Duck: Money coming through all forms of trade.

Eagle: Luck and prosperity through a change of home.

Ear: Interesting news.

Easel: A new job.

Egg: Increase, expansion, new plans and creativity.

Elephant: Good health, luck and increased strength.

Eye: Look before you leap!

Face: A friend comes.

Fairy: A happy love affair. (A fairy will look different to an angel, which is larger and fuller.)

Fan: Flirtation and indiscretion, so be careful.

Fish: Good news and good luck.

Flag: A friend may prove untrustworthy.

Flock: A flock of any type of animal signifies public meetings and large gatherings, whether of family or at work.

Flowers: Love, favours, praise and happiness.

Garland: Love, happiness and honour.

Gate: Opportunities await you.

Giant: Obstacles in your path.

Goat: Enemies and misfortune, especially for a sailor.

Goose: Happiness and a successful venture.

Grasshopper: A good friend will become a soldier.

Gun: Discord and slander.

Hammer: Triumph over adversity.

Hand: Good friendship, loyalty.

Handcuffs: Disgrace, misfortune.

Hare: A long journey, or the return of a friend.

Harp: Success in love and marriage.

Hat: Success in life.

Hawk: An enemy.

Head: A warning of family illness.

Heart: Pleasures to come.

Hen: An increase in riches.

Horns: A powerful enemy.

Horse: Comfort and success.

Horse shoe: Success in marriage, good fortune.

House: Success in business, or a new home.

Initial: Sometimes the reader will get lucky and an initial will be very clear in a reading. It is usually in relation to the enquirer and depending on what other signs are nearby it can mean a range of things – a person's name or a clue to something else - so always read the initial within its context.

Ivy: Happiness and patience.

Jug: Good health and money-making.

Kettle: Illness or even death.

Key: Money and other circumstances improve.

Kite: Travel or a scandal.

Knife: A warning of disaster.

Ladder: Travel and good fortune.

Lamp: Success in business.

Lighthouse: A good sign of security.

Lightning: Bad weather on the horizon so batten down the hatches, as they say.

Lion: Greatness through powerful friends.

Man: A visitor.

Mask: The ending of a love affair, as the truth is unmasked.

Maypole: Small satisfaction in your pursuits.

Medal: You will be rewarded for past achievements.

Mermaid: Misfortune for those at sea.

Mirror: Prophetic dreams - so make a note of them and trust them.

Mouse: Poverty due to theft.

Nail: Toothache and dentistry.

Oar: Sports.

Obelisk: Honour and wealth.

Owl: Avoid anything new.

Palace: Good fortune and favours.

Peacock: Success in prosperity and marriage.

Pear: Great wealth.

Pheasant: Good fortune, perhaps a legacy.

Pistol: Danger, even disaster.

Pyramids: The achievement of honour, fame and wealth.

Queen: Security and peace.

Rat: Treachery, deception and enemies.

Raven: A very bad omen!

Ring: A marriage.

Saucepan: Many troubles lie ahead.

Saw: Troubles brought about by strangers.

Scales: A lawsuit.

Scissors: Illness, quarrels, friction and even separation.

Serpent: Slander and spite.

Shark: Death.

Sheep: Prosperity and success.

Shell: Good luck from an unexpected source.

Ship: A successful journey.

Spider: Money coming.

Square: Restrictions, or a message via a letter.

Star: General good fortune.

Straight lines: Determination needed.

Sun: Happiness, health and success.

Table: Consultations, suggestions received.

Toad: Deceit and unexpected enemies.

Trees: A lucky sign of prosperity.

Triangle: A sign of good luck.

Umbrella: Annoyance and trouble.

Unicorn: A scandal.

Vampire: Sorrow and news of a death.

Vase: Good health.

Wagon: A sign of impending poverty.

Wavy lines: A difficult path.

Wheel: An inheritance.

Windmill: Success in an enterprise.

Woman: Pleasure and happiness.

Yacht: Pleasure and travel.

Zebra: Travel and adventure in foreign lands.

Earth Magic ~ Herbs

Dear Reader,

I discussed a number of herbs in *Spells in the City*. However, there are a couple of herbs that are just so magical that they need to be explained further.

Lavender and sage are two of the most amazing herbs that the earth can give us. A witch's cupboard can never be without them! These two herbs can be used for absolutely everything from cooking to healing, from magic to spell-weaving. Both lavender and sage are from the Mediterranean. I want to describe their very many uses and then in turn you can try and experiment with other herbs, since their properties can be compared, for example, to rosemary or mint. Whatever you try, always remember that although this is 'earth magic' the magic is really within you and it is you who must take ownership of your magical works.

Lavender
The medicinal uses for lavender range from treating migraines (infusions made from the flowers applied as a compress to the head) to an antiseptic. It can also be taken internally to calm anxiety and nervous exhaustion. The essential oil when combined with a carrier such as sesame oil can be applied to treat sunburn, burns and insect bites. If you suffer from tension, or muscle aches and pains, lavender can prove most beneficial in a massage oil. Further, inhaling the fragrance of the flowers or

the oil can be very calming, anti-depressive and can also relieve insomnia.

The ancient Egyptians used castor oil to deter head lice; however something far nicer is lavender essential oil. You can make a wash of it by putting a couple of drops in a bowl full of hot water and then leaving the hair brushes and combs in it to soak. Afterwards, put a couple of drops on the actual brushes and combs and massage it in, then comb and brush the hair as usual; this will help to discourage head lice.

The actual cosmetic uses of lavender are amazing. The infusions of fresh flowers make a fragrant hair rinse. You can also put the lavender in an oat-filled sock and tie this to the tap so that the water runs through the oats and lavender for a soft, comforting bath. Alternatively, you can tie the lavender in bags to scent the bathwater, but the simple way is just to add a couple of drops of essential oil to the bath water. It can also be used in soaps, massage oil, in body lotions and as a moisturiser.

Aromatically, the flowers can be dried and used in potpourri and scented sachets which can be placed in wardrobes and drawers to deter moths and insects. It can be used in candles to give a lovely scent. In spell-weaving, it is one of the main ingredients of love spells as lavender is an aphrodisiac, so it is perfect for love, romance and harmony spells.

When it comes to cooking, the flowers can be used to flower sugar which then can be used for making cakes, biscuits, meringues, ice creams and desserts. The flowers can be added to vinegar, marmalade and jam, or cooked in a muslin bag with blackcurrants or soft fruit mixtures. To make lavender sugar, simply put your sugar in an airtight container and then put some sprigs of lavender in with it, leaving them until you have used all the sugar.

Lavender Marmalade
4 tbsp. of dried lavender flowers, soaked in 50ml of warm water for ten minutes and then strained.
6 oranges
1 kg sugar

Wash the oranges and cut them into quarters, then chop them all up in a blender until finely ground, skin and all. Then boil them up with the sugar and lavender for about twenty minutes, stirring occasionally. Fill sterilised jars with the mixture and screw the tops on, leaving them to cool completely before putting them in the `fridge, where the marmalade will keep for six months.

You can make lavender jam too, with sugar that contains pectin or with special jam-making sugar that you can find in supermarkets. Use three cups of water to half a cup of lavender flowers. Follow the guidelines given with the jam-making sugar. You could also try it with the juice of one lemon. Another good combination is apples and lavender - you could make an apple and lavender jelly. The possibilities with lavender are endless; try experimenting with it and substitute it for other herbs in various dishes.

Sage
Sage is a part of the mint family and is commonly used in cookery with onions and used as a stuffing, yet there is so much more to this wondrous plant. However, like the mint family if it is allowed to grow freely in the garden it will take over, so keep it contained in a pot.

Medicinally, sage can be used as an astringent, an antiseptic and it is antibacterial. Infusions of the leaves can be used as a mouthwash for sore throats, mouth ulcers, gum disease, laryngitis and tonsillitis. Infusions are taken internally as tonics to aid digestion and for menopausal problems. It can also be applied externally as a compress to help heal wounds due to its antibacterial qualities. However, a word of warning about sage: the essential oil is toxic in excess doses and should not be taken medicinally over long periods by pregnant women or by those with epilepsy. Sage is a uterine stimulant, and it can also trigger seizures.

As for culinary purposes, it is quite safe to use in small amounts. While lavender can be used really for a whole host of sweet dishes, sage can be used for many savoury ones. The leaves may be used in drinks or, better still, freeze the leaves in an ice cube tray and use them as flavoured ice in teas and summer drinks.

Sage is a perfect accompaniment for vinegars. Vinegar itself is a wondrous resource for us and no witch's cabinet is without a little jar of it. It can be diluted with warm water to be used to treat sprains and bruises. Further, you can dilute vinegar with iced water to make a good compress for swollen joints or hot tension headaches.

Vinegar hair rinse is great for keeping the hair conditioned. You need to dilute 1 tbsp. of herbal vinegar with 250 ml of water. Rub it thoroughly into the scalp and leave it for five minutes before rinsing out. Herbal vinegars are great and sage is perfect for auburn hair, as sage darkens hair while chamomile or lemon lightens it. Parsley cures dandruff, by the way, while rosemary conditions dry, thinning or falling hair.

Vinegar and Brown Paper
All the children's nursery rhymes have an element of truth in them. Vinegar brings bruises to the surface; it cools and reduces swelling. A vinegar poultice mixed with sage is an excellent traditional combination for easing sprains. You can use a pestle and mortar to bruise the fresh sage leaves, or you can flatten them with a rolling pin. Then put the sage leaves in a pan and cover them with vinegar. Simmer gently for about five

minutes - do not boil. After this time take out the leaves and lay them flat on a cloth - be quick and careful as the leaves will be very hot - then fold the cloth with the leaves inside and apply as hot as possible to the affected area. Cover the cloth with a towel and leave it for an hour or until the swelling has subsided.

Smudge Stick
When it comes to magic, sage is a powerful ingredient in spells. It is one of the main herbs in smudge sticks, which traditionally originated with the Native Americans. Sage was also the key herb for all sorts of things - healing, rituals and magic. Smudge sticks are used to cleanse the air of negativity and to rid the house of unwanted guests. It is perfect for creating a sacred space.

You can make your own smudge sticks and if you are lucky enough to have your own garden you could grow different varieties of sage in different pots. Traditionally it was white sage that was used, but you can also combine it with lavender. Cut the sage in 15-20 cm lengths. You need quite a bundle, bound together tightly with some thread or black or white cotton, and then left for the sage to dry out.

When the smudge stick is completely dry you can use it in your space-clearing rituals. Set light to the end of the sage then blow out the flame and waft the smoke through the air, cleansing the sacred space. There is really no 'right' or 'wrong' way to create sacred space; magic is within you so do whatever feels right for you.

If you feel as though you are not alone at home, or there is something different about your living space, as if perhaps there are 'unwanted guests' there, then try to clear it. Take back your power and reclaim your home. You have all the energy and power you need within you to clear the space. Light your smudge stick then blow out the flame to create smoke and keep blowing into the stick to keep the smoke coming. Go to every room in the house while saying:

> *You are not welcome here.*
> *Power of sage, make all clear.*
> *Unwanted visitors, disperse from this place.*
> *I now reclaim my living space.*
> *Go back from whence you came*
> *And never come back again.*
> *An' it harm none, so mote it be.*

A full description of and guidance about 'unwanted visitors' is given in *Spirit in the City*.

Lavender and sage are two of the most important magical herbs because their uses are endless. In magic they can be used in spells for happiness, healing, health, lust, psychic awareness and money.

There are of course many other herbs that work just as well as these, and new uses are now being discovered for other herbs (though those working in the Craft have known about them for some time). Pelargonium is one such plant that seems to be gaining notoriety now, used to relieve the symptoms of upper respiratory tract infections including the common cold, sore throat, coughs and blocked or runny noses. Pelargonium is basically a geranium, of which there are about two hundred species, so be careful if you are thinking of eating your garden flowers! Always be sure which species it is.

Another form is Geranium Robertianum which grows wild in the hedgerows in Britain. It has many different names including Herb Robert, Red Robin, Stork's Bill, Crow's Foot, Cuckoo's Eye and even Death Come Quickly (though I know it as Bloodwort). If you were reading a two or three hundred year old grimoire, you may see written "2 pinches of Cuckoo's Eye", or "mixed with one part Dragon's Blood". This is not literal! Both terms can refer to the same plant, though Dragon's

Blood can also refer to the sap and resin of the Dragon's Blood tree. It is important to know your herbs.

However, this lovely plant produces tiny pink flowers with five petals which are perfect for practitioners of the Craft who refer to it as "the plant of magic". (Although every plant with five petals will be associated with magic due to the connection with our most sacred symbol, the pentagram.) It is also regarded as a lucky plant and people carry the flower with them to attract luck.

Apart from magic and luck it does have other uses, such as being a remedy for toothache and nosebleeds. It can also repel mosquitoes, so if you are camping especially near lakes and are being attacked by the midges find this flower and rub some of the leaves on yourself. It can be used as a gargle for sore throats and mouth ulcers; it is good for inflammations of the skin and also for diarrhoea. Some also say that this plant boosts the immune system and can help in the treatment of some forms of cancer. It was one of the traditional folk medicines of the Native Americans.

Enjoy your herbs, love and respect all plant life, for magic is a part of them just as it is a part of us.

Blessed Be

Masks

Dear Reader,

The face of the Green Man looms out of trees and from the earth to us here in the west, while in Asia the contented face of the Buddha beams across the land on temple walls. In Egypt the mystical face of Tutankhamen peers through space and time, the epitome of ancient Egypt. There is indeed something magical about all these faces.

Human beings like to look at these symbols, these faces of time and tradition. They bestow something upon us and gazing at these faces we find peace, knowledge and reverence. We honour the cultures and their peoples every time we look into these faces and masks, many of which have magic and myths associated with them. It is said that if you look upon the face of Tutankhamen you will never want for anything, while gazing upon the face of the Buddha will bring you peace.

Ancient priests and tribesmen wore masks to emulate the gods. Masks serve the purpose of distancing the wearer from other people by making one appear strange and mysterious. In magic itself, masks are sometimes worn to aid the invocations of the gods. However, many gods like to change themselves into different things in order to walk among their people. Zeus is one god who changed his identity many times, usually to seduce a new lover, and Odin is known as the god of identity and masks because he often changed his appearance and hid his true identity in order to walk among his subjects.

It is the magic of masks that appeals to us here. The mask is something physical we can wear every day; it shields us from harm or, when we do not feel well, we put on the mask of wellness, the mask of "I am fine". And there are set times of the year when the wearing of masks becomes a national pastime. Hallowe'en is one such time when the wearing of masks seems to be a prerequisite. Hallowe'en, or as we call it Samhain, is a time when the dead come back to the Earth. The masks people wear are intended to change the identity of the wearer and so confuse the spirits of the dead who walk amongst us at this time.

The changing of identity, or of shifting one's appearance into something else or somewhere else, leads us to the magical phenomenon that is astral projection, which is the soul floating free from the body. If we view our bodies as the mask that our soul wears, then our potential as spiritual, magical beings is endless. Astral projection has been written about since the beginning of time. The ancient Egyptians believed that the human soul leaves the body in the shape of a human headed bird, or 'Benu'. Many people who have a 'near death experience' (NDE) speak of astral projection or an 'out of body experience' (OBE). There are many who now believe in the magic of astral projection as a means of gaining access to higher spiritual realms for guidance, and some have learned to train themselves to do it through dreams.

If you wish to learn astral projection, think carefully about it as it can be a very frightening experience at first; waking up on the ceiling and seeing one's body below is quite alarming! However, you can train yourself to deal with this. It is best to perform this when you are in a deep state of relaxation, some say just before dawn or when you have just woken up. It may be best to meditate in order to reach that state of deep relaxation, as you need to reach a kind of hypnotic state. Keep your eyes closed and become aware of your body: think of your hand, your foot and focus on each part of your body. Visualise moving your body but do not physically move it; at this point some people may feel vibrations running through their body as the soul prepares to leave the body. Feel yourself rise up above your body and be totally free from the weight of your body.

It takes a lot of practice to get to this point but the more you practise the easier it will become. Think of it as exercise for the soul. Once you've got the idea of it you can practise going into another room, or going anywhere you so desire. However, no matter how far you go always remember that your soul is connected to your body by a silver cord which is an invisible force; remember that you are in control and if you become frightened you can simply stop and your mind will recall your soul back to the body. As you wake up, wriggle your toes and fingers and allow yourself to regain full consciousness.

Hypnos, the Greek god of sleep, put people to sleep with a touch of his wand or by fanning them with his wings. Ironically the mask of Hypnos is an amazing mask and is quite a beauty to behold. If you can, have an image or replica of it in your bedroom and focus on that while you train yourself to astral project. You could also ask Hypnos to grant you safe passage in your dreams by saying this spell before you go to sleep:

> *Dear god of sleep,*
> *I ask my soul to keep.*
> *Grant me safe passage in my dreams,*
> *Let me wake without screams.*
> *Dear Hypnos, Blessed Be.*
> *An' it harm none, so mote it be.*

Masks, astral projection and dreams fall into one sphere of magic, the magic of identity and character. At the end of this letter there is a brief description of dream symbols. The interpretation of dreams is intricately woven within magic and our everyday lives for dreams are how we work out problems; and as described above, in astral projection through dreams we can train our minds to wake up and allow our souls to take flight.

The wearing of a mask means you can behave differently. When you wear a mask you are shielded from the world and inside it you feel free from the necessity to conform; this is something still celebrated at the traditional carnival of Venice. Some people fear masks but we should embrace them as they are another part of magic; after all, as astral projection shows, the body itself is the greatest mask of all.

Blessed Be

Dream Symbols

Acorn: Great potential for the future lies ahead.

Axe: A warning of cutting back or redundancy.

Baby: The birth of a new idea.

Ball: A ball symbolises the world. It also represents life and the game of life. In fairy tales, the golden ball means greater understanding and also the wonderful gift of wisdom.

Cake: Sweet but transient things are under consideration.

Chair: An empty chair signifies a vacancy. This is a sign of double meaning as it can mean a sad loss or a promotion.

Daisy: This flower is a symbol of love and affection and kindness.

Dog: This always signifies a loyal friend and companion, no matter which breed.

Echo: A warning against repetition.

Elf: A spirit of the elements acting as a dream messenger.

Fence: An inhibiting factor, an obstacle.

Fountain: To see and drink from a fountain is to drink form the healing waters of life itself.

Gold: A precious memory.

Gypsy: To see a gypsy, or a gypsy camp where smoke is rising, warns of a departure in one form or another.

Hair: Virility and attractiveness to the opposite sex.

Hat: Wearing or seeing a hat in a dream relates to the desire for recognition and respect; of course, the crown is the ultimate hat.

Ice: A lack of feeling and sensitivity.

Ivy: Ivy is a hard, clinging plant so beware of hangers-on.

Jellyfish: This creature indicates that a mysterious situation exists which defies logic.

Jug: Life holds more than you realise.

Key: The solution to a problem or the way to happiness. It is the answer to your question.

Kite: To see a flying kite tells the dreamer to be confident and proud of what and who they are.

Lawn: Cultivate a serene and calm outlook.

Leek: Like onions, leeks are signs of good health and of course they are also the symbol of Wales.

Map: Destiny and the future.

Mole: Moles represent spies so beware of those who cannot be trusted.

Naked: Revelation of one's true nature.

Nun: A nun symbolises the wise woman within as well as an especially revered person.

Owl: A sign of wisdom.

Oyster: This shellfish means the world could be yours for the taking.

Pig: A person degraded in the dreamer's eyes.

Primrose: Romantic relationships need careful handling.

Quay: Make the most of the calm before a storm.

Queen: A queen represents feelings of equality and familiarity. She is also Mother Nature.

Rice: Good news is to be expected at home; perhaps also a wedding.

Rope: A strong attachment to someone or something.

Sand: Small annoyances will soon pass.

Sky: The sky is the limit, so be confident and go for that special goal.

Table: An altar upon which self-sacrifices are made.

Tiger: A sign of physical energy, drive and enthusiasm.

UFO: The individual search for inner illumination.

Unicorn: This creature symbolises purity, virginity and compassionate beliefs.

Veil: The truth is hidden from the dreamer's view.

Vulture: Beware of a vicious competitor wanting to move in and take their pick.

Water: Emotions and feelings.

Wolf: A wolf signifies hard times ahead.

X-ray: Unseen forces at work which bring changes.

Xylophone: This musical instrument means you should try to keep in tune with others and life generally.

Yawn: An outlet is needed to escape from a boring situation.

Yew: This tree represents family problems which cannot be altered.

Zebra: This animal represents choice and chance.

Zoo: The world populated by members of the human race.

The Green Man

Dear Reader,

For us all, magic is in every part of our world, but at times it is easier to see it in nature than in ourselves. The Green Man reconnects us with the male energy of the world as we embrace the masculine force of nature. The Green Man can be said to exist within the subconscious of those who love nature, plants, animals and trees. He is nature, he is the forest and he is the tree, he is the animals and he is earth magic at its best. This letter will focus on tree magic.

There is much old lore surrounding tree magic. For example, planting lilac, honeysuckle and almond trees in your garden provides financial stability for the family. However, remember that if it's white lilac you should never cut it and bring it into the house as anything white in nature belongs to the Goddess, no matter how tempting its beautiful smell. Furthermore, silver birch, maple, holly and ash are believed to bring luck to the household, while a monkey puzzle tree is generally best avoided. The elder tree is a very sacred tree and is said to protect humans from the spirit world. However, the poor cherry tree is always said to harbour evil spirits.

Among all the many trees, none is more revered than the mighty oak, a very sacred tree. It is sacred to Thor as that is the tree which is most likely to be struck by lightning. (Thor of course is the Norse god of thunder and lightning.) Also, oak is said to be magical. It is believed that if you carry an acorn with you, eternal youth will be yours. It is wise to leave an acorn on a windowsill as it will ward off storms. Furthermore, if an oak tree has mistletoe growing around it this is said to have special powers; the advice is to cut off the mistletoe with a gold knife on the sixth day of a new moon and catch it in a white cloth, not allowing it to touch the ground as then the mistletoe will lose its power. The mistletoe is then placed in water and the liquid used as a charm to ward off evil spirits.

Horse chestnuts, or conkers, are believed to protect against rheumatism. Horse chestnuts and acorns are used in many spells and the legends of their powers are passed down from generation to generation (many chestnut spells can be found in *Spells in the City*). The hawthorn bush is often used in magical practices, one of our main plants for spells and rituals; it is very sacred to us and we have many customs and legends associated with it. However, unfortunately it is often also used, allegedly, by those who practise 'black magic'. A famous witch trial of 1579 found the accused guilty of murdering four individuals by piercing the left side of a poppet with the spikes from a hawthorn tree.

Hawthorn is officially recognised as a drug in Europe, the USA and India. It has healing properties that are beneficial for cardiovascular disease; it lowers cholesterol and aids digestion. Incidentally, the oxygen that hawthorn releases can eliminate feelings of tiredness and dizziness; it can help with waking up and it eases yawning.

The two main species in Britain are known as the May Tree, English Hawthorn or, as my father knew it, The Bread and Butter Tree! People were known to eat the leaves and flowers to take the edge off their hunger. They are the trees with the tiny, white, slightly scented flowers that bloom in May. Hawthorn was even used as a substitute for tea and tobacco during the first World War, and the seeds were ground and used instead of coffee - an acquired taste.

Hawthorn is one of my favourite plants. In legend it was said to have first sprouted after being thrown in a lightning bolt by the god Thor. In ancient Greece and Rome it was used in wedding decorations as it was believed to increase fertility. We still use it now in our hand fasting ceremonies, from a flower garland made in the spring to a lovely autumn garland or a bouquet made with the beautiful red berries, entwined with ivy and holly at a midwinter wedding. Hawthorn is one of those wondrous plants that brings goodness with it and it was often seen as a symbol of hope. It is said to ward off evil. We use it in our May Queen and midsummer festivals; we decorate the tree with ribbons and people dance round them. In our ancient beliefs, witches were said to transform themselves into hawthorn trees and to hold their rituals underneath hawthorns. Yet in truth, every tree is sacred to us.

The leaves, berries and flowers of the hawthorn can all be dried and will last about six to twelve months, although when fresh they will only last about three days. Pick young leaves for their maximum healing power. There are many things you can make to benefit from this spectacular tree. You could check your local health food store for capsules, essences or tinctures of pure hawthorn, but if you cannot find any then have a go at making a tincture yourself from the leaves, flowers and berries. These are harvested at different times. The flowers bloom in May and you could pick the young leaves then or in April depending on the weather. The berries are harvested in October or November.

Hawthorn Tincture

To make tinctures, use alcohol (high proof vodka) which preserves all the ingredients with no deterioration and kills any bacterial and fungal spores. However, you can substitute this with apple cider vinegar if you do not wish to use alcohol.

Use 225 – 300 g of hawthorn flowers, leaves or berries. Wash them all thoroughly and place them in a blender, covered with the vodka or vinegar. If using the berries, work quickly as they can set in thirty minutes. If the blades of the blender become difficult to turn, add more liquid. Blend all the ingredients until smooth.

Now pour the mixture into a large, sterilised dark jar and cover it with an airtight lid. Give the jar a shake, label and date it, and store it in a cool dark place. After two days, measure the contents and add half the amount again of water, then leave the mixture for at least two weeks (but no longer than four weeks). Strain the mixture through a jelly bag, overnight is best, then pour the liquid into a dark jar, label and date it, and store it in a cool dark place. We would begin this process when the moon is new, then strain and bottle at the full moon, so the whole process takes almost a month. You have now made a tincture. For medicinal purposes, use 1 tsp of the tincture diluted in 5 tsp of water twice daily.

Hawthorn Tea

The other lovely way to take the benefits of the hawthorn is either by a delicious jam or in a tea. I would advise investing in a teapot with an infuser, or you could use a coffee pot with a plunger. However, if you intend to make lots of different teas then I suggest you invest in the right kind of equipment.

Place 2 tsp of hawthorn leaves or flowers in the teapot and pour in hot water, leaving it to steep for five to ten minutes depending on the strength and taste you like. Then press the plunger down and pour the tea. You can sweeten it with honey or by adding a little cinnamon or nutmeg. A lot of these new tastes might be a shock to your taste buds but, as with nettle teas, you do get used to them over time and they are far healthier for you than normal teas. If you use a natural sweetener instead of sugar or artificial sweetener you will notice the difference in yourself after a couple of weeks.

If you intend to pick the flowers of the hawthorn, remember

what has been said regarding anything white in nature. Think of nature as not belonging to you alone. The Green Man and the Goddess must always be respected. After all, you would not go into a shop and just take things of a shelf, would you? The same is true within nature especially where it concerns the white flowers of the Goddess. Therefore, ask permission before picking the hawthorn flowers by saying these words:

> *Goddess of grace, goddess of love,*
> *Thank you for your gifts from above.*
> *Blessed Be.*

Goddess Jam
The other delightful way to take the benefits of the hawthorn is in jam. This jam is delicious and it is relatively easy as it requires no cooking and no extra sugar. Remember that hawthorn berries have a high quantity of pectin so when crushed they set quite solid by themselves in about thirty minutes.

However this jam uses other berries from the bountiful Goddess. This is one for an autumn day, for picking berries in the countryside, although we can also find many of these berries now in our towns and cities.

2 parts hawthorn berries
2 parts blackberries
2 parts elderberries
1/2 part rosehips
Pure vegetable glycerine
Maple syrup

Wash and clean all the berries. I would recommend soaking blackberries and elderberries overnight in salt water to get rid of all the lovely creepies! Then rinse them well and measure all the ingredients. As tempting as it may be to add extra rosehips, do not as they will spoil the texture of the jam. Then place all the berries in a blender and cover with a mixture of half vegetable glycerine and half maple syrup. Make sure all the berries are blended well. If the blades become difficult to turn, add more of the watery berries such as blackberry and elderberry instead of the maple and glycerine mixture as that will just make the jam too sweet. When the mixture is blended and smooth, place it in sterile jam jars, labelled and dated. Unopened, the jam will last about a year in the fridge. However, once opened it should be eaten within two weeks.

A word of warning regarding elderberries: the leaves and stalks contain toxic substances and the berries are harmful if eaten raw, so I would recommend always boiling them up and never eat them if they are not ripe. If you are unsure of the elderberry plant, as some species are poisonous, then substitute the elderberries with blackcurrants which are also high in vitamin C. By the way, the leaves in particular of the elderberry have insecticidal properties. After boiling them in water, this can be used as a spray against aphids and garden pests. Wear gloves when gathering and handling the leaves and always wash your hands after use.

Divination

On Midsummer's Eve, use the hawthorn blossom to foresee the future. Sprinkle some hawthorn flowers over your magic mirror. Light a yellow candle and a black candle and say these words:

> *Blossom might, blossom white,*
> *Gracious lady, thank you*
> *For your gifts this night.*
> *I wish, I may, I wish, I might.*
> *Grant me the gift of foresight.*
> *An' it harm none, so mote it be.*

Look into the mirror and see what unfolds within it. When you are scrying, always make sure you have a pen and paper handy as you will soon forget what you see due to the excitement of seeing into the future.

We respect the Earth, we respect the land, we respect the country. If we are in a city or a town, we respect the nature that is there all around us at all times. It is our duty to care for the Earth, for nature and for all animals. Its magic weaves its way through our lives as it weaves its way through us. The Green Man is regarded as the consort of the Goddess. If our Lady is within the flowers of the hawthorn then our Lord is within the tree. All is connected and all is sacred and all is magical. Every tiny sapling needs to be cared for and nurtured as magic flows through all, no matter how large, no matter how small. We need to be respectful to nature and to the Green Man.

Blessed Be

The Yggdrasil

Dear Reader,

In Norse mythology the Yggdrasil was a huge tree that connected the Nine Worlds of the universe. It was often depicted as a huge ash tree with branches reaching into the heavens and its roots into wells and springs. Further, creatures lived in the tree including dragons and eagles. The eagle and the dragon were arch enemies and their feud was encouraged by a mischievous squirrel that spent most of his day running up and down the tree of life, reporting what the eagle had said about the dragon and vice-versa. Even in the world of magic there is trouble!

The Yggdrasil is where the gods dwell, in a place called Asgard ruled over by Odin and Frigg. The world of humans is Midgard, presided over by Thor. The Yggdrasil has been called 'the World Tree' (or Worlds' Tree). It is complete with all life and magical beings from gods to dragons, from giants to elves and of course humans. The interconnectedness of the World Tree really is the epitome of magic.

Another special magical being lives within the Yggdrasil, called Norns. They can be compared not only to the Three Fates of the ancient Greeks but also the Stygian Witches who feature in the ancient Greek story of Perseus defeating Medusa. Did you notice that special number again; three witches, three Fates, three Norns? The three Norns were very similar to the Three Fates as they are also known as the Goddesses of

Fate in Norse mythology. They spend most of their time spinning the webs of destiny, the threads of life for every living being including humans, animals and even the gods. They are very powerful and are to be revered.

The Destiny Spell
If you feel you need to re-establish your fate, then cast this spell. Imagine what you would like your life to be like; then light a gold candle and say the words below three times over the candle. Imagine the Goddesses of Fate listening; show them how you want your life to be and how you could do it, keeping the images of your intended life in your head.

> *Blessed Be to you, Goddesses of Fate.*
> *Spin me strength, health and love.*
> *Be merciful with me and mine*
> *By your powers of destiny, your powers divine.*
> *Be gentle with my life, be tender with my fate.*
> *Goddesses of past, present and future, Blessed Be.*
> *An' it harm none, so mote it be.*

It is the interconnectedness of humans, animals and gods that the Yggdrasil represents. We are all linked. As the Yggdrasil is the World Tree, then create your own family tree complete with cousins and their children and all family members. Make sure you get their birth and marriage dates, etcetera. See how many people you are connected to by blood or marriage, and how far back you can trace them. We all start somewhere.

Alternatively, you could make a friendship tree. How many people do you know? Who are they married to? When were their children born? Are you a godparent? We are all connected to others either by friendship, blood, marriage or adoption. Also do not forget your pets, for we are all connected, so include the names and dates of pets in your tree of life. Create your tree on paper, or if you would like to create a rustic vintage feel to it then stain white printer paper with a cold, wet tea bag and leave it to dry. You can always attach another sheet with glue when you need to add more family or friends. Then role it up like a scroll and tie it with a pink, purple or red ribbon, and keep it somewhere safe. It is something to add to with every new arrival, every new marriage, or with every passing, and then pass on in your family.

Family Protection Spell
Here is a specific spell of protection for your family or friends that you can perform. Write out the names of your family or friends, or use your family tree scroll if you have made one. Have the names in view as you light an orange candle and say these words:

> *Bless this family, bless this home,*
> *Wherever we may wander, wherever we may roam.*
> *Let our love shine throughout our family.*
> *Let us be safe and protected wherever we may be.*
> *An' it harm none, so mote it be.*

The Yggdrasil is symbolic of the interconnectedness of all, the Tree of Life. If you have a Yggdrasil anywhere in your garden then why not literally create a family or friend tree? Attach little cards to its branches of your family and friends with their picture on one side and their name and birth date on the back.

The Yggdrasil is the World Tree of all creation, yet it also links us to the spiritual world, the cosmic centre which lies within everyone and exists everywhere at once. Another term for this is the Axis Mundi which literally means sacred space, the point where Heaven and Earth meet. In art, the Axis Mundi is often depicted as a tree very similar to the Yggdrasil. A further description of the Axis Mundi and its spiritual aspects will be given in *Spirit in the City*.

Blessed be

Magic and Miracles

Dear Reader,

In the last letter we learned how connected we all are and about the beings that live within the Tree of Life. There are also other types of beings we are connected to, such as the angels. In this letter we shall look specifically at the angels of miracles, and the role of magic in the miraculous.

When we see something amazing happen, we are lost for words. Some people immediately believe it's a miracle while others think it's coincidence. Yet what is a miracle but something that happens which we cannot explain? The same could be said of magic! In reality, magic and miracles are one and the same, although witches believe that magic is something we can manifest while a miracle is numinous. Magic comes from us, while a miracle is from the divine.

Miracles are the spiritual manifestation of our needs and desires made whole. They do happen; if you do not believe in miracles then how can you believe in magic? In your Book of Shadows, or a diary, write down unexplained events that have happened in your life: how you got out of a tricky relationship or situation, or how you got better from an illness. Think about all the difficult moments in your life and how they changed to bring you where you are now - and what you are reading right now. You picked up this book so there must be reason for it…

As the Yggdrasil showed, we are all connected and we all have a guide or someone who walks beside us. They are there when we need them the most. Angels feature very strongly within magic. Indeed there are angels of magic; all angels perform miracles but some feature more predominantly than others and have more encounters with miracles and magic.

The planet of magic is often regarded as Saturn, whose angels are Astel, Bachiel and Sammael. Saturn rules Saturday and the angels of Saturday are Cassiel and Tzaphiel. The true angels of magic are Zaphliel, Zadkiel and Camael (though some believe the angel of miracles is Hamied). Of course, all angels are powerful in their own right but one in particular who can be counted on for everything is Gabriel.

> *Gabriel, help me please,*
> *Send your help in whomever you feel.*
> *Thank you.*

We believe that angels are always with us though they will not help us unless we ask them to. So just remember Gabriel when in need and call upon him - or her, an angel can often appear as a female. Normally, angels are a very bright light with no form as such, filling you full of love, warmth and happiness. If, however, in the presence of this light you feel sadness, pain or anger, then wherever you are get away from that place for we do not work with 'those ones'.

The signs that angels are around us are, of course, finding feathers unexpectedly but it may also be coins. For many years I often found two pence pieces as signs that the angels are around. When it comes to magic and miracles, always trust your initial instincts, that 'gut reaction' we speak of. Your first response is the one you need to go with. Learning to trust your instincts takes time but you can ask for guidance and help from your guides and angels.

To learn to connect with your inner voice, it's good to meditate and to be still and quiet. It is very hard to do in our busy lives but you do need to have some 'me, myself and I' time. On an evening when you will be alone, lock the door and turn off 'phones, computers and televisions. Make sure you will not be disturbed. Light a purple candle and create a protected sacred space or circle. You can either create a small circle which you will be in by summoning a circle, or you can spray holy water (which is sea salt and water). You can create sacred space by placing five crystals that you feel close to evenly around you in a circle. Imagine a wall of protection around you generated by the crystals and the holy water. (I taught how to create a sacred circle in *The Witch in the City*). When you have created your sacred space and your candle is lit within the circle, then sit down and calm yourself, close your eyes and focus on your breathing. The other way of entering a meditative state is by visualisation of a special place or by focusing your gaze on an object such as the flame of the candle. When you are content that you are now in a peaceful state, say this spell:

> *Great Spirit, help me to be wise and true.*
> *Let the right action come through.*
> *Help me to listen to your voice.*
> *I will listen now that I am free.*
> *Speak words of instinct and of wisdom.*
> *An' it harm none, so mote it be.*

Afterwards, sit or lie down in the circle and listen to your inner voice come through. Think of a problem you have and what you should do about it. You must let yourself be totally relaxed. Listening to your instincts does take a while to learn so do not be too disappointed if you receive no ideas at first; you must continue with the meditation ritual and exercise the spirit. Remember what was previously written: magic is not always easy, some parts of it are difficult while other parts will come naturally.

One aspect of magic that appears to us all and not just to believers is miracles. Miracles feature throughout the ancient world and many of our world religions describe miracles that have resulted in a festival honouring it. The Festival of Lights known as Hanukkah is one such. The angel of miracles made sure the temple lamp oil was replaced each night and so with very little oil the lamp was lit for eight days, for the rededication of the temple (in 165 BC).

In our modern history there have been many miracles for which the Earth breathed a sigh of relief. One such moment was the Cuban missile crisis of the 1960s. This situation could have ended in the complete annihilation of every living being on this planet. A miracle, or just good politics? You decide. Another famous case of angelic miracles was at one of the first major battles of World War I, the battle of Mons. On the 24th of August, 1914, as the British began their retreat at Mons, there appeared angels who protected the retreating British servicemen. The Angel of Mons has become a legend in spiritual circles and there are countless books written about it. The Great War became a turning point in world history, for never before had the world seen such carnage. Yet it was a war in which magic and miracles featured very strongly. One other such battle of importance was the Battle of Argonne. The Meuse-Argonne Offensive was fought by the brave men of the 308th Infantry in the October of 1918. As a result of this battle, the allies were able to break through the German lines and five weeks later, on the 11th day of the 11th month at the 11th hour, peace came.

Let's look at those numbers again. The first major battle of World War I was accompanied by the Angel of Mons on the 24th August, 1914. If we break down the 'magical numbers' we have:

2 + 4 + 8 + 1 + 9 + 1 + 4 = 29

2 + 9 = 11

The 308th Infantry gives us:

3 + 0 + 8 = 11

The Battle of the Argonne Forest resulted in the Armistice at:

11.11.11
And the year peace came was 1918:
1 + 9 + 1 + 8 = 19
1 + 9 = 10
1 + 0 = 1

One cannot help but remember, as mentioned earlier in this book, the writing of Hebrews 11.1: "Faith is being sure of what we hope for and certain of what we cannot see." Nothing could be truer of peace at that time.

The number 11 features predominately throughout great times in history. Is it a coincidence, magic or miracle? Eleven is the number of human experience. It is the link between mortal and immortal, between darkness and light, between ignorance and enlightenment. Nothing could be more appropriate with reference to the Great War - sheer carnage and loss of life on a scale never seen, and wars were never fought that way again.

Blessed Be

Gods and Goddesses of Magic

Dear Reader,

No book on magic would be complete without mention of the great goddesses of magic and witchcraft. There are three main goddesses, also the most popular ones: Isis, Diana and Hecate. Yet there are also two other goddesses who are to be considered equal when it comes to magic and the Craft. They are Aradia and Morrigan. These form the pentagram of the great goddesses of magic and witchcraft.

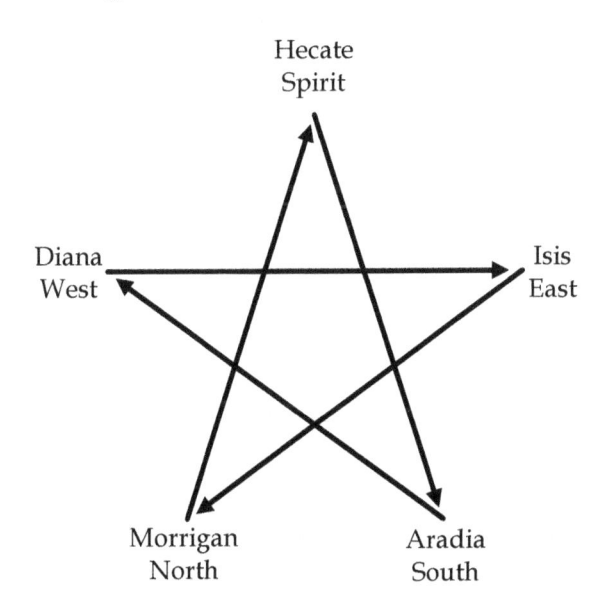

```
                Hecate
                Spirit


Diana                           Isis
West                            East




      Morrigan          Aradia
      North             South
```

We shall look at each of these lovely yet powerful (and sometimes frightening) goddesses. Decide which one you are akin to the most - mine are Morrigan and Hecate. All of them come from different cultures which you may feel attracted to. If this is the case, then it could be a past life influence or you could be interested in a certain aspect of that culture or of that particular goddess. As always, trust your instincts and let your inner voice be your guide. If none of these goddesses of magic and witchcraft 'speak to' you, that is also fine. You are in control of your own path and your own magic will be your guide.

The Goddess with You
If after reading about each of these goddesses you cannot decide which one(s) to work with specifically, then try this spell. Each goddess represents a point on the pentagram and has a corresponding colour and element.

Hecate	Spirit	White
Isis	East	Blue
Diana	West	Green
Morrigan	North	Yellow
Aradia	South	Red

Light the candles of each of these colours and say these words over them:

> *Hecate, Isis, Diana, Morrigan and Aradia,*
> *Mother goddesses of magic and witchcraft,*
> *I will listen to you at last.*
> *Show me which of you I shall serve.*
> *One or all I shall work with and deserve.*
> *Blessed ladies, show me please.*
> *An' it harm none, so mote it be.*

Sit still and watch the candles. The one whose flame withers and goes out or splutters and judders down represents the goddess for you.

Aradia

The Italian goddess of the witches, she is the daughter of Diana and came to Earth to impart her knowledge of magic and witchcraft to us. She is credited with creating witches. Being the first witch of the world, Aradia was able to teach her practices and secrets to others who therefore became the first coven.

There are many practices that have developed as a result of the worship of Aradia, with rituals, ceremonies, invocations and incantations addressed to her. Practitioners also held meetings with incantations over the honey, meal, salt and wine cakes at a witches' supper (very similar in many respects to what was practised in classical Rome). The herbs that are sacred to Aradia are vervain and rue; the cakes are made of rye meal, wine, salt and honey which are then formed into the shape of a crescent moon. Wholemeal rye flour (widely used in Roman times) is used to make dark rye bread - try your hand at making it if you feel a connection to Aradia.

In the goddess pentagram, Aradia is the south and is associated with fire, for she is the eternal flame of magic and witchcraft. Her colour is red for the fire and for the blood of the martyrs of witchcraft, the thousands of brothers and sisters who were punished for practising magic and healing in the past (and undoubtedly in the future too).

Aradia Crescent Moon Cakes

1 cup of wholemeal rye flour
1 cup of honey
3 tbsp. of red wine
3 tbsp. of salt

Mix all the ingredients together, shaped into a crescent moon. Preheat the oven to 350 °F (180 °C, Gas Mark 4). You can either line a baking tray with greaseproof paper or wrap your crescent moon cake in greaseproof paper to cook so that it keeps its shape. Put the cake in the oven for thirty minutes (but check after twenty minutes). It will naturally be dark in colour so do not assume it has been cooked through; check it with a skewer - if the skewer comes out clean when stuck into the thickest part of the cake, then it is cooked. Leave it to cool.

Then light a red candle, have a glass of red wine or grape juice, and put some sea salt and honey as well as the cake on your altar. Give thanks to the goddess for choosing you to work with.

Diana

The Roman goddess of hunting and of the moon, she was also known as Artemis in ancient Greece. Diana is often prayed to and revered by practitioners of magic, regarded by those who worship her as the first goddess of magic, created before all creation. In her were all things, light and dark.

Diana, like her daughter Aradia, taught magic and sorcery. Diana became known as the Queen of Witches after she showed the fairies, goblins and other magical folk that she could darken the heavens and turn all the stars into mice. She herself could change her form into that of a cat.

To find a stone with a hole in it (now often known as a hag stone) is a special sign of favour from Diana. If you find one, give thanks to Diana on the night of a full moon:

> *Blessed Be, great Diana,*
> *Queen of Heaven and of Earth,*
> *Protectress of all.*
> *Thank you for your gift.*
> *Thank you for my magic.*
> *Blessed Be, great Diana.*

In the goddess pentagram, Diana is in the west and her colour is green (as goddess of the Earth). Diana is Roman and here in the west the Romans are responsible for many aspects of society we have today. Congratulations if Diana has chosen to protect you in the great work of magic.

Hecate
Although a goddess, she is also part of the 'Triple Goddess' of Greece. She is the goddess of the Underworld and is associated with crossroads. Hecate (or Hekate) is probably the most mysterious and feared of the goddesses of magic, being fearless herself; she was the one who, on hearing that Hades had whisked Persephone away to his home in the Underworld, grabbed her twin flame torches and went to get Persephone back, which she did. Unfortunately, as Persephone had already eaten the seeds of death, she had to spend months of the year in the Underworld, each seed representing one month. After this time, Persephone could then spend the rest of the year with her mother, Demeter.

Hecate, goddess of illumination, accompanies Persephone for the months when she is in the Underworld. We know this time as winter. As Hecate spends half the year in the Underworld, she is both of the light and the dark. She is often depicted with her three-headed dog, the heads representing past, present and future. A black dog is her symbol, as are snakes, keys, torches and a white dress. If you dream of or see a black dog in spirit form, it could mean that Hecate is trying to connect with you.

In the goddess pentagram, Hecate's throne is in spirit for she is the essence that moves through all. She is the summer and winter, she is the light and the dark. She is loyal to her followers while at the same time can be extremely forbidding to her enemies, a force of love and a force to be reckoned with. Her colour is the white of spirit but, through the prism, white light reveals all the colours.

If Hecate is the goddess who has chosen you, be respectful and honour her by always having a white and a black candle on your altar. If you can, also buy a clear quartz crystal and dedicate it to Hecate. Clean the quartz either by soaking it in salt water for an hour or by wafting a smudge stick over it. Light the candles and say these words:

> *Goddess of dark, goddess of light,*
> *Blessed Hecate, make it right.*
> *This quartz I give to you.*
> *Imbue it with your love and grace.*
> *Help me to make the great work of magic.*
> *In your honour I shall work.*
> *Mighty Hecate, Blessed Be.*
> *Great Hecate, thank you for choosing me.*
> *An' it harm none, so mote it be.*

In your magic work from now on, when healing or spell-casting, always have your quartz crystal to hand.

Isis

The Egyptian 'Great Mother' was worshipped throughout the whole of the Roman world, for Isis does not just belong to ancient Egypt. Her spell-casting powers are second to none. After her husband Osiris had been killed and cut into fourteen pieces by his brother Set, the parts distributed all over the world, Isis found all but one of them and brought her husband back to life with a spell. Notice that fourteen is 1 + 4 = 5, the number of the pentagram, the symbol of magic.

Yes, the one missing piece was *that* one! Yet for a powerful magical goddess, this didn't seem to matter as she then conceived a son with her reborn husband. So Isis is the mother of Horus, the god of the sky and the national patron god of Egypt.

Isis and her followers can still be found all over the world. She has an enduring appeal for many practitioners of the Craft and for those who simply like her image. The everlasting appeal of the ancient Egyptians hits home to many people living today. Are the people of those times returning once again to us? If you have a kinship with Egypt then it is highly likely your goddess is Isis.

In the goddess pentagram, Isis is in the East; she is blue and associated with water (for the Nile). Her stone is the beautiful blue lapis lazuli, and her symbol is the tyet, or 'knot of Isis', similar to the ankh. Her flowers are roses.

If Isis is your goddess, then give thanks by creating a ritual of cleansing and purification. Make a ritual bath with 5 drops of essential rose oil in your bath water, then soak and meditate in the bath. If you do not have a bath, then put 5 drops of essential rose oil into your shower gel and shake it up. After your ritual bath or shower, light a blue candle and say these words:

> *Mother Isis, thank you for working with me.*
> *Blessed waters of the Nile,*
> *Wash me clean and cleanse my soul,*
> *Pure for evermore.*
> *For the great work of magic is sought.*
> *Mother Isis, Blessed Be.*
> *An' it harm none, so mote it be.*

Isis is the Great Mother and a great goddess of magic, so it is a great honour if she has adopted you. Be respectful and always give thanks by placing a rose or two on your altar when good little things happen to you.

Morrigan

The Celtic goddess of battles, strife and death, she is often regarded as 'the Triple Goddess' of Ireland. She is the one we pray to when we are confronted with struggles and confrontation. To have Morrigan fight on your side is a great honour. Although at times she can be vindictive, she is a fearsome and strong goddess and a great ally to have. She is also known as the goddess of the circle of life as she is associated with both birth and death.

Morrigan is also referred to as the Phantom Queen, possibly due to the fact she is also a shape shifter, appearing in many forms. One of these is the crow or the raven which are her animal symbols. If you constantly see a crow no matter where you are, town or city or countryside, then it is highly likely that Morrigan is letting you know that you come under her watchful gaze.

Her sacred plants are Mugwort, yew and willow. In the goddess pentagram she is to the north. As Aradia is in the south and linked to Italy, so Morrigan is in the north and linked to Ireland. Her colour is yellow and her element is air, due to her shape-shifting abilities. She is everywhere and nowhere, for the shape shifter constantly reinvents herself and can adapt to any environment.

There is another term in magic similar to shape shifting, called 'glamour'. Originally a glamour was regarded as a spell cast by a witch to make somebody see things in a different way, but it later came to refer to a spell which literally changes a person's appearance. If you have a battle coming up, a job interview or any challenging meeting, and need to glamour and portray yourself as strong and confident, the best and the victorious, then cast this spell. Light a yellow candle and say these words over it:

> *Gracious Morrigan, I call upon you.*
> *Change me so that only I can see*
> *The nature hidden within me.*
> *Let my appearance be strong and true.*
> *I am confident and right to those who view.*
> *Great Morrigan, Blessed Be.*
> *An' it harm none, so mote it be.*

These are wonderful goddesses of magic and I hope you enjoy working with them as much as I do. It is a true honour to work within the realm of magic. But never take liberties with it or use it for the wrong purposes. Always remember our code:

An' it harm none, do what ye will,
Lest it return threefold.

You have been warned!

Blessed Be

The Last Word

Dear Reader,

We have now come to the end of our journey into magic. We have delved into the depths of magical squares, symbols, music and masks. We have learned the practices of tea reading and astral projection. We have focused on two herbs in particular, lavender and sage. The reason for looking in depth at the herbs in particular is to show you how wondrous and magical the earth truly is, that something so small can have so many benefits and uses. We look beyond the obvious and we find the magical.

This brought us to the magic of miracles and how truly wondrous they are. We have gone back in time to two different wars to find the magic that was present even in the darkest of times. There is always light for there is always magic, no matter how hopeless things appear to be.

Therefore, dear Reader, realise your potential, unleash your power and embrace the magic that is within you.

Blessed Be

Suppliers of Excellent Resources as used by Tudorbeth

Here is a list of magical suppliers that I have used and can highly recommend. They are run by wonderful people who will give you first class service and will always be helpful. They are simply my magical pentagram of resources.

Animal Unicorn Healing ~ www.animalunicornhealing.com
This is run by a natural earth witch who specialises in working with and healing animals. Her animal healing waters and elixirs are handmade for each animal.

Cosmic Unicorn ~ www.cosmicunicorn.co.uk
A sparkling jewel in the witchcraft crown; everything the modern witch would ever need or want.

Eloise Kirlan's Magical Shop ~ www.eloisekirlan.com
Wonderful hand-blended oils for every occasion and ritual and, for that matter, every spell you will ever need.

Everything Lavender ~ www.country-stitches.co.uk
The Lavender Lady creates wonderful products from lavender home grown at her cottage in Lincolnshire.

Quest ~ www.spiritualquest.co.uk
58a The Ashley Centre, Epsom, Surrey, KT18 5DB

An Aladdin's Cave of magical resources, complete with everything from angels to music, incense to a fabulous array of crystals.

If you have enjoyed this book, you will like...

The Craft in the City
First in this series, *The Craft in the City* will teach you everything you need to know about witchcraft in the modern world. Here, the essentials of the Craft and of Wiccan beliefs are condensed into a series of easy-to-read letters, in which the author describes spell-weaving, candle magic, the nature of ritual, how to make potions and much more. (ISBN 978-1-907203-43-5)

The Witch in the City
Tudorbeth teaches, in her simple and down-to-earth letters, what it really means to be a witch today. Here she unfolds the secrets of Bell, Book and Candle and the mystical pentagram. She opens up to us the ceremonies of Initiation and Hand Fasting, and much more. (ISBN 978-1-907203-63-3)

Spells in the City
Who has not lit a candle for a loved one, or offered up a devout wish for some important event? Who has not believed in some lucky charm or spoken an affirmation? We are all practitioners of the Craft! So would you like to know how to do it properly, with real natural power and intent, and to get results? In this ground-breaking book, Tudorbeth opens up the traditional secrets of spell-weaving and adapts them for our busy modern lives as never seen before. More than one hundred real and practical spells for you to use now. (ISBN 978-1-907203-70-1)

Further details and extracts of these and many other beautiful titles may be seen at *www.local-legend.co.uk*